# In Search of An

# Old Clay Road ...

Photographic memories of wonderful times on Prince Edward Island
(PEI), the birthplace of Confederation & Canada's smallest province
(2018-2021)

Nancy Dupuis - The Writer in Me

Order this book online at www.trafford.com
or email orders@trafford.com

Most Trafford titles are also available at major online book retailers.

 **www.trafford.com**

**North America & international**
toll-free:  844 688 6899 (USA & Canada)
fax: 812 355 4082

Our mission is to efficiently provide the world's finest, most comprehensive book publishing service, enabling every author to experience success. To find out how to publish your book, your way, and have it available worldwide, visit us online at www.trafford.com

ISBN: 978-1-6987-1198-0 (sc)
ISBN: 978-1-6987-1197-3 (e)

Library of Congress Control Number: 2022909921

Print information available on the last page.

Trafford rev.05/26/2022

# Preface

*Death - 7 short weeks after diagnosis!*

*Leave - once retired and the future that was to be, was no more*

*Face first in Nova Scotia, on the East Coast - I knew not a soul*

*Write it out - the storyline begins for 'Begin Again' by the Writer in Me*

*Infatuation sneaks in – that wasn't in the plan*

*Come home to what – a false sense of happiness?*

*Mom dies - my world crumbles once again but this time the man is still here, very much alive and in my face with apparently no future*

*Go - back to the little Island on the East Coast I knew so well from years ago*

# Acknowledgement

To those who welcomed me so wholeheartedly upon my arrival back on the Island that fall; new friends and old, I thank you from the bottom of my heart.

The photographs I have chosen for this little book are ones that held special meaning to me as I drove the back roads – there are so many more wonderful spots just waiting for your own visit to this beautiful little Island.

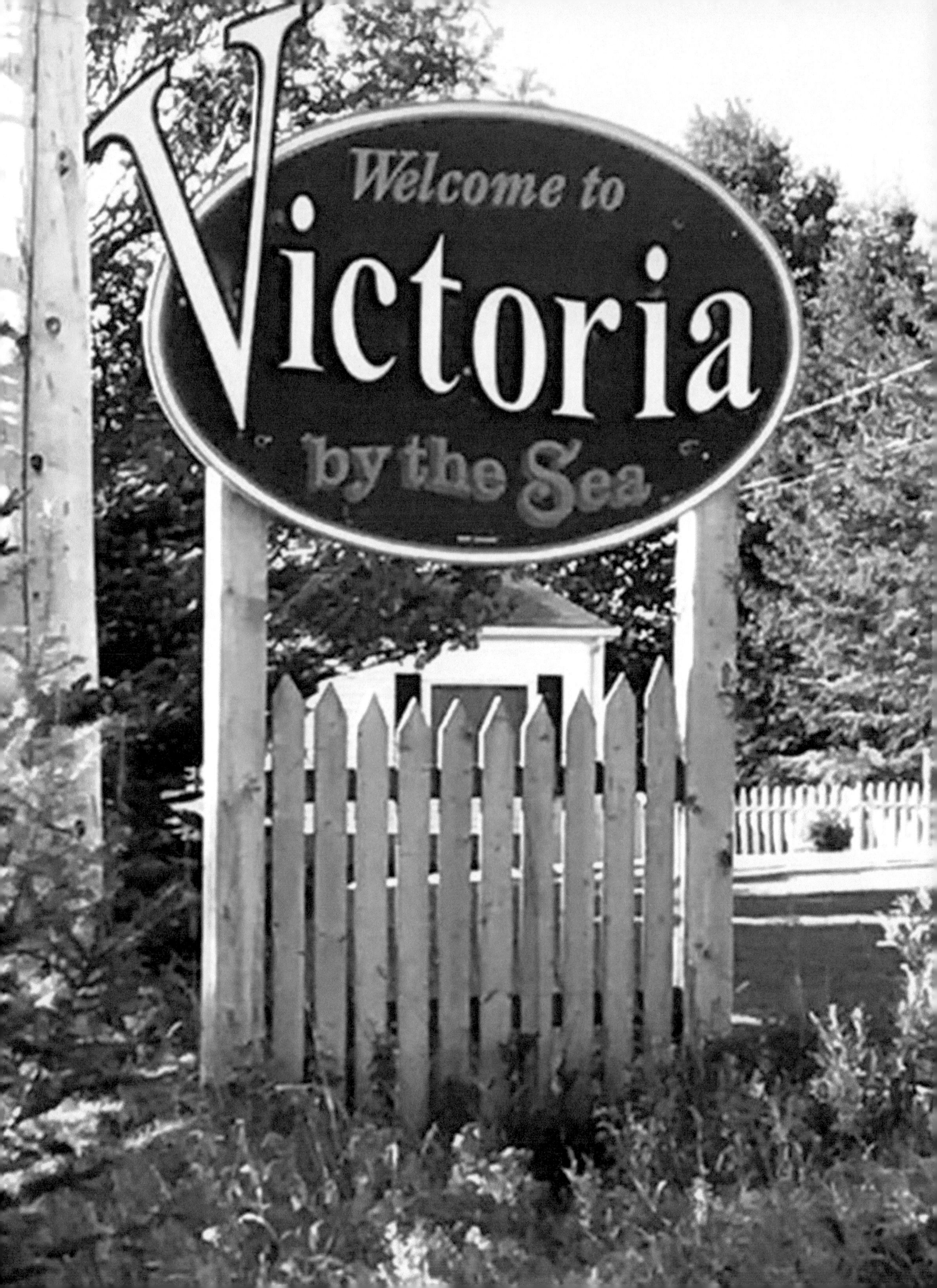
Welcome to
Victoria
by the Sea

# September 2018

*A* screeching need to shed the past for a bit and strike out anew, yet once again; wondering what awaited as I stopped at the side of the road to snap a picture of the sign welcoming all to the village, I was not disappointed. Friendships were made forever in this little village, with a rich history in shipbuilding, fishing and of late - a quaint tourist destination.

I quickly immersed myself in getting to know the people and also to volunteer with some of my spare time. Drawn to the water, I went often to the wharf to capture just a little of the ever-changing skies.

But the most enjoyment has been found travelling the backroads, reacquainting myself with the Island from our time spent here years ago (1991-1998).

*A* beautiful brown lab kept me company in the house I was so fortunate to share; early morning breakfast will never be the same without this little fella waiting patiently behind me at the Island just in case there might be a crumb or two left on my plate – egg, peanut butter on those crusts, maybe?

# The 4 Seasons at the Iconic Lighthouse in Victoria, PEI

*It is noteworthy to say, Victoria was one of Prince Edward Island's busiest seaports back in the day.*

*Scenes from my walkabouts in the village, this first photo depicting the spring colour of the lupins;*

*P*reviously the Wright Brothers General Store, now home to Island Chocolates;

*the everchanging scenes at the wharf;*

*An invite to just sit and dream …*

*B*ut wait … then, I became a tour guide (quite unexpectedly\) for a company serving the many cruise ships arriving at the Charlottetown Port! Wow - I learned so much about the Island and looked forward to the next season with such excitement in sharing my story of why I love the Island so much, being not from the Island – but – being an Islander by choice!

*All set to go on a walking tour;*

*S*upporting Tourism - Cruise Ships at the Charlottetown Port;

*t*he start of a walking tour through Confederation Landing Park in Charlottetown;

*a scene in downtown Charlottetown, part of the walking tour; these doors actually opened for large animals entering the veterinary facility inside long ago;*

*And then, onto those rolling hills, fishing wharfs, back dirt roads and much more;*

*Near French River, PEI;*

*Fisheries, Malpeque Harbour, PEI;*

*P*otato fields outside the village of Victoria, PEI;

*And it's beautiful red shores (the island soil is red, a result of high iron-oxide content);*

*t*his beautiful old church just outside Kensington, now the
home of a great concert site, famous for its acoustics;

*W*hat would a tour of the Island be without a trip to visit Anne of Green Gables;

*L*overs Lane and the Haunted Wood await, as well as a tour of the house;

*A beautiful morning sunrise just coming on at Rustico;*

*T*he Doucet house in South Rustico is possibly the oldest dwelling
on PEI with the original wood frame dated back to 1768;

*The original Farmer's Bank, operating from 1864-1894 was an important link in the establishment of "Les Caisses Populaires" in Quebec and "Credit Unions" in the rest of Canada;*

*And right next door;*

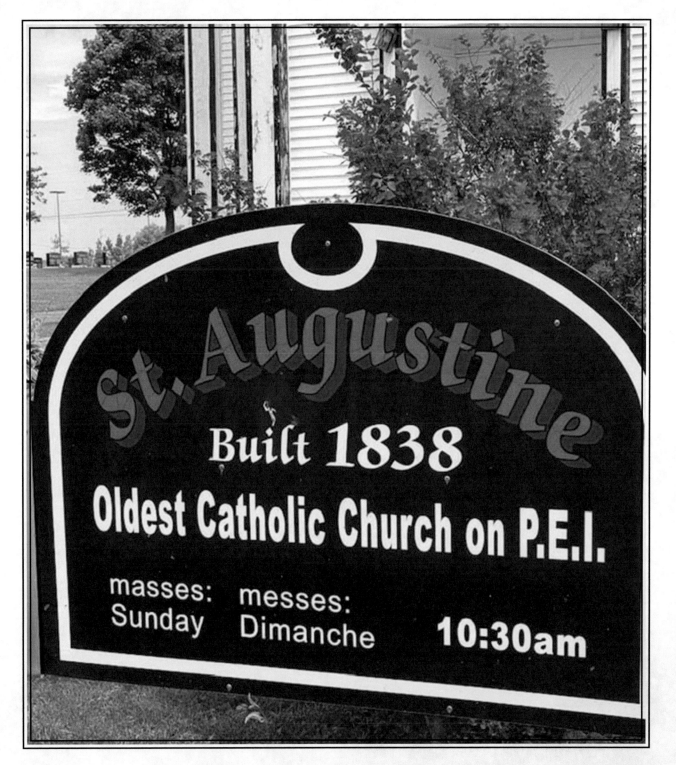

*The Confederation Bridge, linking PEI to the rest of Canada;*

*I*ndian River, PEI

*T*hunder Cove, PEI;

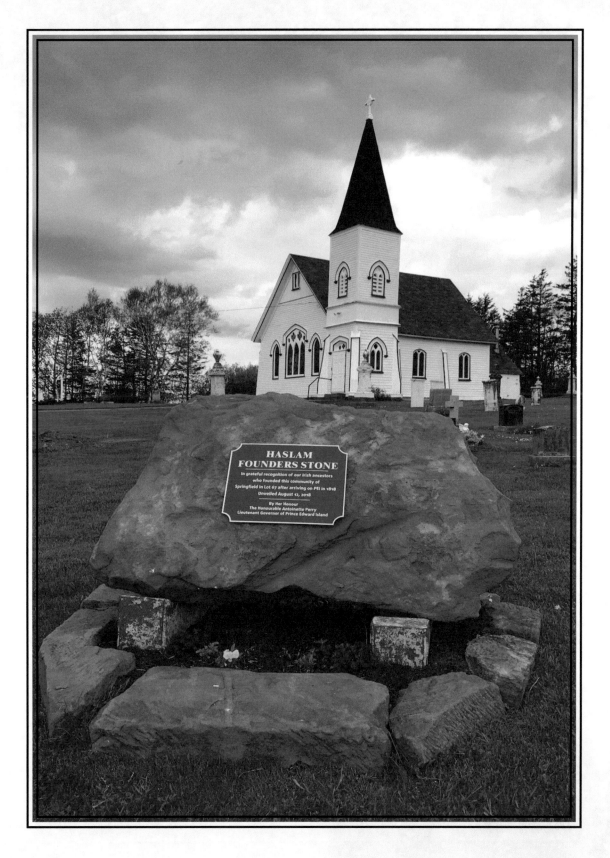

*A* commemorative stone was unveiled during the 200ᵗʰ anniversary of the Haslam family settling on PEI at the church in Springfield, in 2018. The stone comes from the original quarry owned by Thomas Haslam.

*B*uilt in 1881, for a Methodist congregation, Tryon United Church was designed by
William Critchlow Harris, one of Prince Edward Island's most distinguished architects.

*Spring or fall at the Prince Edward Island Preserve Company
in New Glasgow, PEI, one is never disappointed;*

And off I went up another dirt road to explore; what a time I have had on the Island, but now something is pulling me back home.

Thank you to this beautiful little Island and its people who welcomed me with open arms, helped me heal yet once again and just be myself. I am forever grateful for your many kindnesses and generosity; I will never forget my time here.

# About the Author

## Nancy Dupuis – The Writer in Me

Recently relocating home to Almonte, Ontario (September, 2021) I am currently employed at a retirement home here in town and enjoy immensely the personal contact with others on a regular basis, especially during this time of Covid. I am also part of the Communications team for the Scottish Society of Ottawa, currently engaged in writing a monthly series on the impact of the early Scottish Settlers to this area almost 200 years ago. This spring, I have had the privilege of being appointed as a volunteer to the Almonte Bicentennial Working Group to assist in the Bicentennial celebrations in the Mississippi Mills area in 2023. This again, ties in with the settlers arriving here 200 years ago and I can only imagine there are many stories to be told as we celebrate their part in our history.

I was privileged to have been the wife to a military man, thus allowing me to travel this great country back and forth a number of times over his career and for my own opportunity to have worked almost 30 years in the Federal Government as an administrative sort, with the last 13 years of my career as the Special Events Coordinator to the Canada Revenue Agency. After retirement, I began heading out on road trips; some big, some small but all with great impact on the future – again, travelling this wonderful country, finding my niche for writing and taking photographs; eventually self-publishing two books with more on the way.

"Begin Again" is an intimate story about unsurmountable grief and the power in following your heart. It will resonate with anyone who is coping with loss and provides hope for the future.

"Where is Home?" is a further chronicle to my life after the trauma of my husband's sudden passing, now 16 years ago. With the self-publishing of both of these books, I hope my story will help readers recognize the difference between existing and truly living again.

Another couple of books are due to be self-published later this year, the third book called "In Search of an Old Clay Road … and the fourth titled "60 Odd Years". A fifth book "Faith, Hope and Possibility is also in the works.

I take great pleasure in putting my thoughts to paper. I suppose one could call this series "Life after Ray" – something I never saw coming; however, I honour his memory and our life together by being open in sharing my deepest thoughts as I move forward day by day, month by month, year by year now alone, but not defeated. Life is a series of twists and turns – it is how we react that will define us.

Contact info:
Email: nancydupuisisthewriterinme@gmail.com

Printed in the United States
by Baker & Taylor Publisher Services